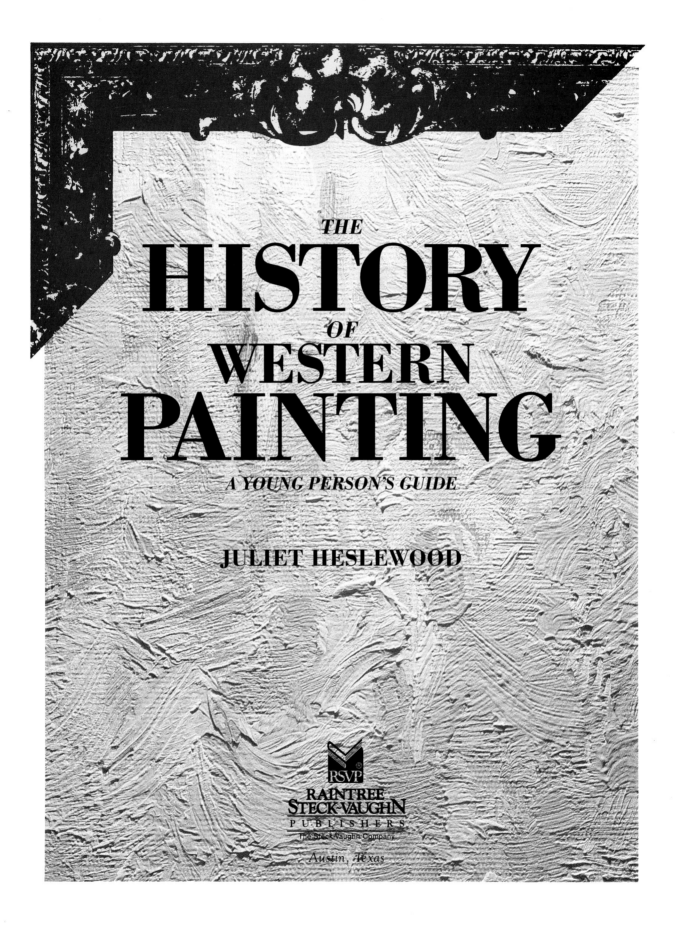

# THE
# HISTORY
## OF
# WESTERN
# PAINTING

*A YOUNG PERSON'S GUIDE*

JULIET HESLEWOOD

RSVP
**RAINTREE
STECK-VAUGHN**
PUBLISHERS
The Steck-Vaughn Company

*Austin, Texas*

© 1996, text, Steck-Vaughn Company

Original text © Juliet Heslewood 1993

Published by Raintree Steck-Vaughn
Publishers, an imprint of Steck-Vaughn
Company

Editors: Jill A. Laidlaw, Shirley Shalit
Designer: Simon Borrough
Picture Researcher: Ann Usborne
Consultant: Susan Wallington

**Library of Congress Cataloging-in-Publication Data**

Heslewood, Juliet.
    The history of Western painting : a young person's
guide / Juliet Heslewood.
        p.   cm.
    Includes bibliographical references and index.
    Summary: Presents an overview of Western painting
from ancient caves to the modern world and includes
information on artists.
    ISBN 0-8172-4000-4
    1. Painting—History—Juvenile literature.
[1. Painting—History.]   I. Title.
ND50.H52   1995
759—dc20                                     95-11428
                                                  CIP
                                                   AC

Typeset by Tom Fenton, Neptune, NJ
Printed in Singapore
Bound in the United States
1 2 3 4 5 6 7 8 9 0 LB 00 99 98 97 96 95

**Cover pictures: left to
right, Benozzo Gozzoli,
detail from *Adoration
of the Magi* (see page 16),
1459-61; Leonardo
da Vinci, *Mona Lisa*,
1503 (see page 18);
Vincent van Gogh,
*Self-Portrait*, 1889
(see page 52).**

*For my sister Jennie*

**Photographic credits**
Artothek 28 center left; The Board of Trinity College,
Dublin 11; Bridgeman Art Library 20 left, 23 top left, 25,
26, 27, 28 top left, 30 top and bottom, 36 left, 38 bottom,
38/39, 43, 44, 45, 47 center right, 48, 49, 51 top, /Collection
of Mrs. John Hay Whitney/© Succession H. Matisse/DACS
1994 54 top, /DACS 1994 55 left, /ADAGP, Paris and
DACS, London 1994 55 bottom right, /ADAGP, Paris and
DACS, London 1994 56, /Demart Pro Arte BV/DACS
1994 57 top, Pollock-Krasner Foundation/ARS, New
York 58 top right, /Andy Warhol Foundation for the
Visual Arts 59; /Collection Robert Leber Paris © ADAGP
Paris and DACS, London 1995 57 bottom; Régie
Municipale, Cabrerets 4 left, 5; Mary Evans Picture
Library 8 top left, 9 bottom left, 34 background, 36/37,
41 top; Giraudon 28 bottom left, 31 bottom left, 50 right,
51 bottom, 52 bottom, cover and 52 center, 53 bottom;
Michael Holford 6; The Hutchison Library 53 top left;
The Iveagh Bequest, Kenwood (English Heritage) 29;
Roy Lichtenstein/DACS 1994 58 bottom left;
Sammulungen des Fürsten Von Liechtenstein 34 right;
Magnum/Abbas 38 top right; Magnum/Martine Franck
41 bottom right; Magnum Harry Gruyaert 30/31 back-
ground; Magnum/Erich Lessing 7, 28 bottom right;
Mansell Collection endpapers 46/47 background, Musée
National D'Art Moderne; The National Gallery, London
17 top right, 22 right, 24, 35 top, 46; National Galleries
of Scotland 53 top right; The National Trust 31 bottom
right; Nippon Television Network Company, Tokyo 20
right; Museo Nacional del Prado 37 right; Museo
Nacional del Prado/DACS 1994 54 bottom 1993;
Réunion des Musées Nationaux cover and 18 top right,
35 right, 42; Scala 8 bottom left, 9 top, 12, 13, 14, 15,
cover and 16, 17 bottom left and right, 21, 23 bottom left
and right, 32, 33; Frank Spooner Pictures 4 right, 10;
Jonathan Stephenson title page, contents page, 47 top
right and bottom right, 50 background, 52 left; The Tate
Gallery 47 bottom left; The Tate Gallery/ADAGP, Paris
and DACS, London 1994 55 top, /ARS, New York 58 center right; Reproduced by permission of the Trustees of
the Wallace Collection 40, 41 bottom left; Vincent van
Gogh Foundation, Vincent van Gogh Museum,
Amsterdam 52 top; Windsor Castle, Royal Library 1994
Her Majesty The Queen 18 top and bottom left, 19.

# Contents

**1: The Ancient World**
Cave Painting 4
Greek Vases 6
Roman Walls 8

**2: The Middle Ages**
Painting Christ 10
The Frescoes of Giotto 12
Altarpieces 14

**3: The Renaissance**
The Artists of Florence 16
Leonardo da Vinci 18
Painters for the Popes 20
The Artists of Venice 22

**4: Outside Italy**
The North of Europe 24
Painting Imagination and
  Real Life 26
Rembrandt 28
Indoors and Outdoors 30

**5: Popes and Royalty**
A New Kind of Painter –
  Caravaggio 32
Rubens 34
Velázquez 36

**6: Peace and Revolution**
A Classical Past 38
Rococo Delights 40
Revolution! 42
Goya 44

**7: Changing Landscapes**
The English Land 46
The French Land 48
Monet and the Impressionists 50
Painting the Colors of
  the Sun 52

**8: The Modern World**
Picasso and Other Wild
  Beasts 54
Dada and Dreams 56
New Frontiers – America 58

Glossary 60
Further Reading 63
Index 63

Words found in **bold** are explained
in the glossary on pages 60-62.

# 1: THE ANCIENT WORLD

## Cave Painting

The earliest paintings have been found in caves all over the world. **Prehistoric** people lived at the entrances of these caves and the paintings are deep inside them. There are pictures of the animals they hunted, such as bears and fish. From these paintings we know about animals that are now extinct like the **mammoth.** There are also painted images that are more difficult to understand – odd geometric shapes or colored dots. The paintings appear on the walls of the caves or sometimes high up in their roofs, where the rock surface is smooth. The size and shape of the rock often helped the painters' ideas. A large area might be just right for a pair of bison or a long stretch of wall would do well for a herd of horses.

### How was it done?

The paintings were cut into the rock and then filled in with paint. Paints were made from earth substances, like rocks and plants that gave them their red, yellow, and black colors. These paints were ground into powder and kept in hollow bones that were plugged at one end. Animal fat was used to make the paint liquid. The paint was put on the walls with a brush of leaves and twigs, a pad of fur and moss, or else fingers were used.

This prehistoric painting is known as *The Circus Horses* because the horses look as if they have leaped out of a circus ring. From Pêch-Merle, France, c. 18,000 B.C.

The young men who found the caves at Lascaux.

### Accidents

The caves of Pêch-Merle (France) were discovered by accident in 1922. Two young men were exploring the original entrance used by prehistoric people. The famous Lascaux caves (France) were found by four boys who had gone in search of some legendary treasure. Fresh air and pollution have partly destroyed the paintings, so a new imitation version of Lascaux has been built in order to preserve the original.

Both men and women "signed" the walls of their caves. You can tell which hands are female because the wrists are smaller.
Pêch-Merle, France, c. 18,000 B.C.

## Handy Hints

In many prehistoric caves images of hands appear. The painter placed his or her hands on the wall and blew paint over them. The same images have been found in ancient **aboriginal** art in Australia, thousands of miles from Europe. Are they a kind of signature, or simply a doodle? Was it to say that people were now here, where once animals had lived in the same cave? **Archaeologists** are still trying to find out the meaning of these hands.

# Greek Vases

We know how the ancient Greeks painted from their many vases that have survived. The Greeks also painted their walls but few examples have survived. Vases were used as cups, mixing bowls, wine coolers, perfume flasks, and as **memorials** for tombs and graves. These vases were always carefully and beautifully decorated.

The earliest vases (1100–800 B.C.) had simple geometric patterns that went around the shape of the vase in repeated bands (see left). These changed later into more adventurous designs including flowers, animals, and people. Stories in Greek **mythology** of heroes, heroines, and their deeds replaced the patterned bands. These adventures can be read like a book running around the vase.

## Black and Red Figures

Pottery was painted in what is now called the black-figure **technique** (700–400 B.C.). The shape of the figure was spread in black paint onto red clay and detailed lines were cut into the vase by scratching the surface. The figures look like silhouettes or photo-negatives.

Later (530 B.C. onward), the red-figure technique was used. This was much more like straight-forward drawing. The outline was drawn onto the vase and the background was filled in with black.

## Skilled Painters

The more the Greeks practiced the art of painting on vases, the more they learned. A flat surface didn't have to have a flat-looking figure on it. The human body was drawn from different angles. Gestures and expressions

The earliest type of vase decoration is shown here in this geometric design. *Attic vase, 740-720* B.C.

6

## The Ancient Greeks

Between 1100 and 500 B.C., the Greek civilization grew into a complex and advanced society. This time in history is known as the period of **Classical Greece.** The Greeks organized their country into small independent city-states. A city-state was like a small country based on a city with its own government and laws. The Greek legal and political system was based upon government by the citizens and many modern Western European systems of government follow some of the same ideas.

The Greeks have also influenced Western architecture, art, the study of medicine, mathematics, and history. We know much about these people from their buildings, tools, art, carvings, sculpture, and writings.

**A black-figure cup from Thebes (fifth century B.C.) showing Ulysses (a Greek leader during the Trojan war) at sea on a raft made out of two pots.**

**A red-figure vase showing Greek heroes fighting. Fifth-sixth centuries B.C.**

could show the feelings of the heroes and heroines. Soon, individual painters of vases were known and appreciated for their partic- ular way of working. What the Greeks achieved in painting and sculpture was copied by later artists.

# Roman Walls

## Volcanoes and Painting

In Italy in A.D. 79 the volcano Vesuvius erupted. Its lava covered the nearby towns of Pompeii, Herculaneum, and Stabiae, which were caught in time and preserved. These towns were not uncovered until the eighteenth century. The walls of the houses at Pompeii and Herculaneum tell us much about the way wealthy Roman citizens lived. Just as we choose wallpapers, posters, and matching colors for our homes, so the Romans carefully thought out their own **interior** design schemes. They painted their walls with frescoes (see box). Sometimes they chose landscape views that showed an **ideal** countryside. Beautiful temples and houses are shown with people walking by contentedly looking about them. The Greeks painted scenes from their mythology on vases and the Romans painted similar stories in their homes and temples.

**A print of the *Eruption of Vesuvius*, as imagined by J. Didier, 1872.**

**This floor from Naples in Italy shows the great skill of the Romans in mosaic work.**

## Pliny

Pliny the Elder was one of the earliest known historians of art. He lived from A.D. 24 to 79. Pliny wrote many encyclopedias, including one on natural history. In this encyclopedia he included a history of painting in the section on rocks because painters' colors were made up of ground-up rocks and natural substances. Pliny's encyclopedia tells us a great deal about the art of Greece and Rome that we would not know otherwise. Pliny died during the eruption of Vesuvius.

**A portrait of Pliny made in 1584 by an unknown artist.**

## Paintings to Fool the Eye

The Romans liked to show their love of nature as well as of heroic tales. The real world is seen in Roman **still life** paintings. Bowls of fruit, animals, fish in baskets, pots, and vases – all are included. The Romans used their skills to imitate exactly the details of the surrounding world. Painters used a special **illusion** effect called *trompe-l'oeil* which means "to fool the eye" in French. Sometimes they covered walls with large, architectural features, like windows or arches – to make it look as though you could really see through the wall.

## Mosaics

The floors of wealthy Roman homes were decorated with **mosaics.** Tiny pieces of colored stone were embedded in the floor to make **decorative** patterns and pictures. The Romans were very pleased with this method and made it popular throughout their empire. Wherever they conquered they laid mosaics.

# 2: THE MIDDLE AGES

## Painting Christ

A detail of Christ from the frescoes in Cappadocia (see below left).

### Christ in Art

Jesus Christ was born in the time of the Romans and people who believed in him were **persecuted.**

In A.D. 324 the Roman emperor Constantine made Christianity an official religion of his empire. He moved the center of his power from Rome to a town in the east of the empire called Byzantium (present-day Istanbul in Turkey). Over the following centuries Christian art flourished there and some of it was called Byzantine after the town.

The period of history from the fifth century to the fifteenth century in Europe is called the Middle Ages. The Christian Church was very powerful and united Western Europe under its teaching. Large churches were built and their wide, curving **vaults** were decorated with mosaics. Light shone brilliantly upon tiny pieces of colored glass and gold. The walls were often painted with frescoes.

### The Art of Icons

In early Christianity, important figures from the Bible had to be easily recognizable images or **icons** – like a president's or a queen's head on a coin. People believed that these images were so holy that the paintings themselves could work miracles. They thought a picture of Christ was not just a likeness, but that Christ was actually living in the painting.

This form of worship was later thought to be wrong. In the middle of the eighth century paintings, mosaics, and frescoes were attacked. The destruction continued for over a hundred years until it was again believed that an icon or image of Christ, the Virgin Mary, and the Saints encouraged Christianity.

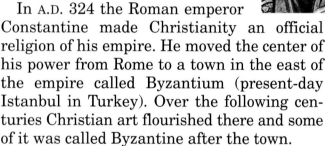

This ceiling of an ancient cave in Cappadocia in present-day Turkey is painted in Byzantine style.

### Stained Glass

Windows in churches tell the stories of Christianity. Small pieces of colored glass are held in place by lead frames. As the building of churches became more daring (tenth century onward), with higher ceilings held by strongly supported walls, so the window space increased and designs became more exciting and elaborate.

Nails are hammered into the lead supports surrounding each piece of glass in a stained glass window.

10

## Painted Books

In many monasteries religious books were carefully painted by hand. Fancy capital letters, delicate borders, and rich yet tiny illustrations to the text were all produced by the monks. When printing was invented, this art gradually declined as greater numbers of books were produced by machine rather than completely by hand.

**Scottish monks painted this page from the *Book of Kells* in the early ninth century.**

# The Frescoes
# of Giotto

## Giotto

Byzantine art spread from the East and was well known by Italian artists. In Italy at this time (thirteenth century) lived a Florentine painter called Giotto (1267–1337). Legend says that as a boy he sketched his father's sheep on a stone. The drawing was so good that he was encouraged to become a painter.

In 1305 Giotto was asked by a rich merchant to work in his newly built family chapel in Padua, near the city of Venice. All the walls of the Arena Chapel were to be covered in religious paintings. Giotto was free to do as he pleased with the subjects of the lives of Christ and the Virgin Mary.

Details of angels from Giotto's *Lamentation*. Lamentation is the title given to mourning the death of Christ.

## The Artist and Storytelling

Giotto needed to be able to tell a good story. He divided the stories into bands of individual pictures, rather like a comic strip. Each picture needed a strong **composition** to explain what was happening. Features like a rock, a tree, or a figure had to be carefully placed so that people looking up at the wall from below could understand what they saw.

Although he had many helpers to put up scaffolding, to mix paint or plaster, and to fill in large areas of color, Giotto did the most important and difficult parts of the frescoes himself. The faces and their expressions came from his knowledge of human nature. Like the boy studying his father's sheep, Giotto studied how things looked. His figures have sturdy, round bodies and their clothes fall in deep folds. This was very different from the decorative style of Byzantine painting that was popular in Italy at the time.

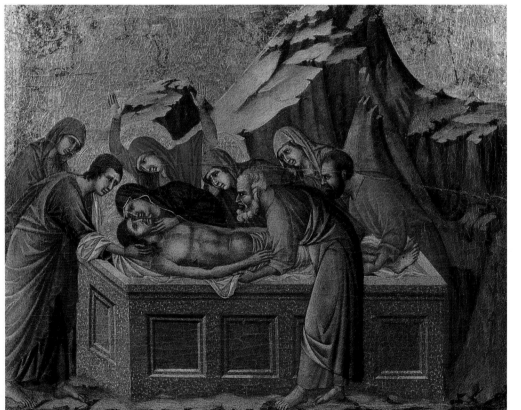

Giotto painted people's clothes to look as though they move around solid bodies in a realistic way (left). *The Lamentation* from the Arena Chapel, 1304–1311.

At the same time as Giotto, the Sienese artist Duccio was still painting in a flat, more iconlike Byzantine style (above). Duccio, *Lamentation* scene from *The Maestà* (see next page), 1308–1311.

### First Sketches

In order to judge how a large fresco would look, a sketch was done on the first layer of plaster with a reddish substance called **sinopia.** This also became the name of the sketch itself. The artist would then fill in a whole area of the sketch on the wet plaster and try to finish that area in one day before it dried.

The face and hands of this figure from Giotto's *Lamentation* are very lifelike.

# Altarpieces

Most people who lived at the same time as Giotto did not know how to read or write. When people went to church they looked at the pictures around them to understand their religion. Christian churches were built in the shape of a cross to remind people of the cross that Jesus died on. The church altar and its platform became important parts of the building. To help people think and pray, the altar soon had its own painting called an altarpiece. Altarpieces illustrated stories from the Bible like the **Annunciation,** the **Nativity,** or the **Adoration of the Shepherds.**

## Duccio's Altarpiece

The Italian painter Duccio (d. 1319) who lived in Siena, not far from Giotto in Florence, won the admiration of his town for his huge altarpiece *The Maestà* – the Madonna and Child with angels surrounding their throne (see below). Small pictures of other scenes surround it and he painted still more scenes across the back (see bottom of page 15). Duccio knew people would walk around the altarpiece. It was specially made for Siena Cathedral and was carried there through the streets in a triumphant procession.

### Golden Paintings for Churches

An altarpiece was made from wood. The framed parts were often elaborately carved and painted gold. The flat areas for images were carefully prepared with an even, chalky surface to prevent the wood from soaking up the paint. The colors were usually mixed with egg into a paint called **tempera.** Finishing touches were added with real gold or silver beaten very thin and applied with glue. This could then be cleaned or polished to a brilliant shine.

*The Maestà* used to have seventy panels but some have been lost. One side of the altarpiece is like a record of holy people (below) and the other side shows scenes from Christ's death (right). Duccio, *The Maestà*, 1308–1311.

Gentile's main story fills the larger shape and below it are scenes from Christ's early life. Gentile da Fabriano, *Adoration of the Magi*, 1423.

## Gentile's Altarpiece

Gentile da Fabriano's (1370–1427) *Adoration of the Magi* (above) shows how the painter of an altarpiece used many ideas. The crowds come in procession through the arched frames, right around the front to the **foreground** of the scene. Colors in the costumes dart across the picture – blues here, reds there. The altarpiece is flat and **two-dimensional** but Gentile shows that in painting you can try to imitate the **three-dimensional** world. By the end of the fourteenth century painting was becoming much more adventurous.

# 3:THE RENAISSANCE
## The Artists of Florence

### Italian City-states

Much of Italy was divided into small city-states ruled by merchant princes. These princes were not the sons of kings, but of rich and powerful trading families. Wars often broke out between them.

Florence is a town in the Tuscan hills that was famous all over Europe for its cloth. One

This is a scene from a wall painting in a Medici family chapel in Florence. Benozzo Gozzoli (1421-97), *Adoration of the Magi, 1459-61* of Florence's most influential families, the Medici, wanted to be remembered as did other powerful families living there.

Powerful families asked artists to paint and sculpt and build for them, and Florence became a center of artistic activity. Schools of learning were created where the books of the Greeks and Romans were read. Soon Florence was thought of as a new Rome – the Classical world of the Greeks and Romans was reborn. This time in Europe from the early fifteenth to the late sixteenth century is called the **Renaissance** which means "reborn" in French.

Artists were encouraged and competitions were held to see who would build churches, decorate palaces, and paint portraits. Many artists tried to do something new.

## Perspective

Frescoes, altarpieces, and palace paintings are all flat and two-dimensional. How do you paint the space inside the picture? How do things appear to be in the distance? Artists studied the science of **perspective** in order to make their pictures look more realistic – as though there were a three-dimensional place there, giving the picture depth.

## Art about People and Nature

Art was no longer created only for the praise of God. People gave themselves a new importance in the world. The Florentines tried to show the world of beauty that was created by God for human beings. The hilly Tuscan landscape outside Florence and its river, the Arno, were studied. The nature, appearance, and thoughts of people were also studied.

## Workshops – Schools for Artists

In a workshop a master painter could teach his craft and the pupil would help the master in his work. Traditionally, artists were thought of as only craftsmen, but by the end of the fifteenth century to be an artist was a great honor. The city of Florence was proud of its independence and power and this was shown through the work of its artists.

Paolo Uccello (1397-1475) applied the new rules of painting to his pictures. This battle is filled with strange colors and figures that seem unnatural and posed. Spears, fallen horses, and hedges are placed to make you look into the painting. *The Battle of San Romano,* 1454-1457.

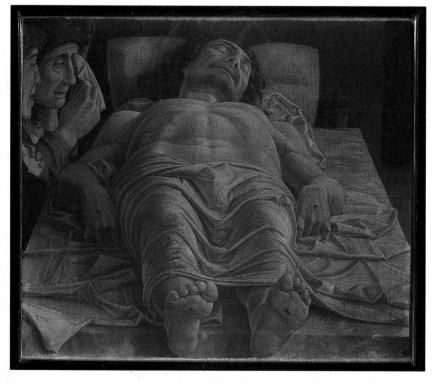

Lorenzo was one of the most important members of the Medici family (above).
Giorgio Vasari (1511-74), *Lorenzo the Magnificent,* c. 1530.

Mantegna showed he understood perspective by placing Christ's body at an unusual angle (left).
Andrea Mantegna (1430/1-1506), *Dead Christ,* 1466.

17

# Leonardo da Vinci

Leonardo depended on noblemen and members of European royal families for work and they often needed new weapons designed. *War Machine*, c. 1487.

Lisa Gherardini was a great beauty. Her portrait has come to be known as *Mona Lisa*, 1503.

During the century that followed Giotto, Italian art was compared to that of Classical Greece and Rome. Leonardo da Vinci (1452–1519) and Michelangelo Buonarroti (1475–1564) are two great names in the history of art and both of them came from Florence.

## The Young Leonardo

In 1472 Leonardo became a pupil in the workshop of the Florentine painter Andrea del Verrocchio (c. 1435–88). Verrocchio gave up painting because Leonardo, his young pupil, was so talented! Leonardo learned most from what he went out to discover. He followed people in the streets and sketched their expressions. He watched the movement of the Arno River and compared it to the movement of the clouds.

Leonardo became well known early in his career. He left the workshop of Verrocchio after only three years of his seven-year apprenticeship. Leonardo was taken into the powerful and important court of the Medici (see previous pages). Although he had the influential prince Lorenzo de Medici for a **patron** (see portrait on page 17), Leonardo always found time to work at his own ideas. He was restless and searching and often did not finish what he had begun.

### Stealing the *Mona Lisa*

Leonardo's *Mona Lisa*, was once stolen by a man who occasionally worked at the Louvre Museum in Paris. He put it under his overalls and walked away. He wanted the painting to return to Florence. When he offered it to an art dealer there, two year later, he was arrested and sent to prison for seven months.

## Leonardo's Study of Nature

Drawing helped Leonardo to discover and explore. Before Leonardo put paint onto the canvas he had already planned and drawn the whole composition, even paying attention to the picture's **tone**. Drawing was the best way he could make notes. He also wrote and drew in many notebooks on everything from war machines to the anatomy of horses. Leonardo studied human anatomy to understand the workings of the body. He was able to paint what he saw accurately—but he also painted with imagination. A distant landscape or the gentle smile on someone's face were all carefully put onto canvas by Leonardo's sensitive touch. He believed that light and shade should blend together without outlines on a canvas as if made of smoke. This effect is known as *sfumato* which is the Italian word for soft.

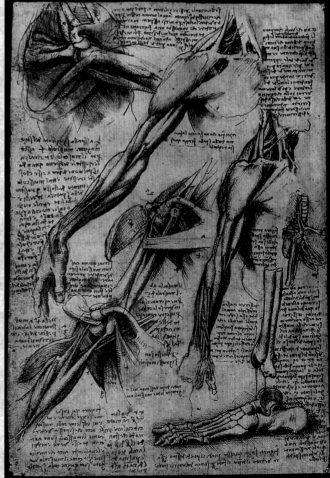

These *Grotesque Heads* (c. 1494, details) are like notes on people's expressions.

Leonardo cut open dead bodies in order to study how the body works. *Anatomical Study*, 1508.

Leonardo felt that if he understood how the body works inside then he could draw it more accurately from the outside. *Anatomical Study*, 1510.

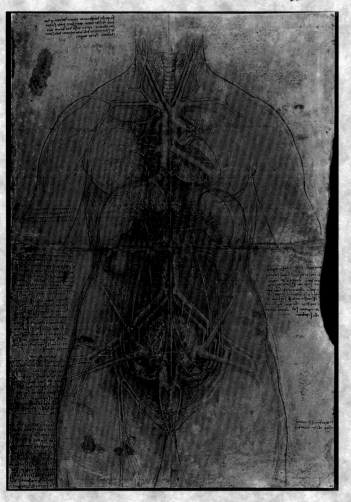

# Painters for the Popes

The popes lived in France for most of the fourteenth century. When they returned to Rome early in the fifteenth century they brought with them money and power. These new Roman popes were ambitious, energetic, and often corrupt men. They had a vision of Rome as the center of the Christian Church on Earth. Instead of tidying up the ancient ruins of Rome, where weeds grew and sheep lived, they started to turn Rome into a fabulous and powerful new city.

## The Pope and Michelangelo

In 1473 Pope Sixtus IV started to build the Sistine Chapel in the **Vatican,** as the pope's private chapel. Sixtus asked the country's best artists to decorate its walls. Much later, in 1508, his nephew, Pope Julius II (see portrait above), decided to change the chapel ceiling. Julius was a man of action who wanted things done well and at once. The young Florentine sculptor, Michelangelo, had been designing a grand tomb for Julius so that he would be remembered after his death. Julius now asked Michelangelo to abandon the tomb project to paint the ceiling. Michelangelo refused by saying that he was not a painter but a sculptor. Julius and Michelangelo often quarreled – especially as Michelangelo worked so slowly – but at last he agreed to paint the Sistine ceiling frescoes. Michelangelo worked almost entirely alone on the ceiling from 1508 to 1512.

## The Ceiling

Scenes from the Old Testament of the Bible spread out high above the chapel walls as if they had been created in the clouds. The painted figures seem sculpted – their strong, muscular bodies reaching, writhing, or wrestling with their thoughts.

**Julius II was one of the most important patrons during the Renaissance.**
*Pope Julius II*, Raphael, 1511–12.

**The Sistine Chapel ceiling is covered with scenes from the Old Testament of the Bible. Michelangelo painted large figures that show the power of the human body.**
*The Prophet Isaiah*, detail from the Sistine ceiling.

**Raphael's Vatican wall paintings show his skill in interior design because each picture had to fit into a specific space.**
*Justice Vault*, **Vatican, 1509.**

# The Pope and Raphael

Julius II was a patron who could always spot a promising talent. He heard of another young painter called Raphael (1483–1520) and commissioned him to paint over the pictures in the pope's private rooms in the Vatican. Michelangelo hated Raphael and claimed that everything he painted had been inspired by his own Sistine frescoes. The spirit of competition between Italian artists and cities that was present at the beginning of the fifteenth century was still alive at the start of the sixteenth century. It helped to create some of the world's finest treasures.

## St. Peter

Christ gave Simon the **Apostle** the name Peter, which means rock. Peter was with Christ on the important occasions of his life. Christ said he would build his church upon his rock—and gave Peter the "keys of the Kingdom of Heaven." Peter was imprisoned in Rome, released by an angel, and later crucified upside-down. He is known as the first pope. St. Peter's is the famous church in Rome that was built by different architects over 150 years. In art, Peter is usually shown with his keys. Saints are usually illustrated with an object relating to their lives.

21

# The Artists of Venice

Venice seems to float on the sea. The sunlight above its buildings shines onto the water, giving the city a warm, sparkling glow.

The Venetian artist Giovanni Bellini (1430–1516) added his own vision of the Venetian light to the same subjects that were known in Florence. His *Madonna and Child* is separated from the natural landscape where country life is seen – yet the whole picture is lit from the same rays of light. We feel a sense of distance because of these various light effects. The overall tone of the painting, with its bright colors, is gentle and warm.

## Bellini's Pupil – Titian

Giovanni Bellini had several pupils including the great artist Titian (1485–1576). Titian often painted Bible scenes as if they happened in the Venice of his own time. He could show how light and color might help to express human feelings. Titian also put new life into portrait painting. The faces are pale against the darkness, yet their clothes are often sharp and clear, with rich colors in contrast. As an old man Titian could make a drama out of any theme he chose, whether religious or mythological.

**For centuries portraits have served the same purpose as photographs. We can tell a great deal about this man from his rich clothes and sensitive expression. Titian, *Man with Blue Sleeve*, 1511–12.**

**A detail of the doge taken from Tintoretto's painting on the opposite page.**

22

# The Art of Jacopo Tintoretto

In the paintings of Tintoretto (1518–94), it is possible to see how much Venetian art had changed by the end of the sixteenth century. A feeling of light and movement could sweep across paintings–not just on canvas, but on the high walls of many of the beautiful buildings in Venice. Tintoretto might exaggerate a table's length or the gestures of the figures, but he was proving how he understood many of the new painting techniques.

Giovanni Bellini, *Madonna and Child*, 1510.

The doge (the ruler of Venice) is shown meeting the Virgin and her heavenly company in Venice. The doge's palace (left) and St. Mark's Basilica (right) are in the background. Tintoretto, *The Doge Kneeling before the Virgin and St. Mark*, 1581-84.

### Giorgione

Giorgione (1477–1510) was also a pupil of Bellini and a great friend of Titian. He knew that he could create a mood by his use of light and color. In his mysterious painting *The Tempest* (left), we ask ourselves, who is the naked woman feeding her baby? Why is a clothed man watching her? Where are they–in a real landscape or an imagined one? Is this an **allegory?** The deep blues and greens of the storm help to add mystery to this puzzling picture.

# 4: OUTSIDE ITALY

## The North of Europe

The Renaissance did not happen only in Italy. In the North of Europe in Holland and Germany, artists looked at themselves and the way they lived with the same new spirit of freedom as the Italian artists and scholars – but their art was very different.

In Florence, rich, large frescoes decorated the walls of many new churches. Painting in the North of Europe was often on a small scale. Sumptuous, elaborate manuscripts were painted for rich dukes who, like the Italian merchant princes, wanted to have their names remembered throughout history. Smallness, beauty of detail and decoration became the characteristics of Northern art.

### Jan van Eyck

Jan van Eyck (d.1441) painted portraits, private scenes, and many altarpieces. He perfected the newly created technique of oil painting, which allowed greater detail to be painted. The pattern and color of rich fabrics, the glow of light upon metal, distant streets, cold stone, tiny jewels – he examined them all in detail and carefully recorded what he saw. The huge *Ghent Altarpiece,* a **polyptych,** with many folding wings, contains three hundred and thirty heads. Pliny (see page 9) said that if an artist painted a hundred faces, many of them would be the same. But Jan van Eyck's angels look so individual that he seems to have known them all personally!

This wedding portrait of a couple inside their home is by Jan van Eyck. You can see the artist painting the scene in the mirror on the wall in the back of the room. The writing says "Jan van Eyck was here." *Giovanni Arnolfini and his Wife,* 1434.

24

Albrecht Dürer (1471–1528) was one of the greatest artists of the Northern Renaissance. Dürer is famous for his amazingly detailed drawings, etchings, woodcuts, and engravings.
*The Apocalypse* (detail, right), 1498.

We do not know the name of the person who painted this altarpiece. Historians have called him the Master of Flémalle because at one time it was thought that he came from Flémalle in Belgium.
*The Mérode Altarpiece* (left-hand panel), c. 1425, Master of Flémalle (no dates known).

## Painting Familiar Things

To paint a world that was recognizable and familiar was what these artists hoped to do. A saint might be painted living in an ordinary home. St. Joseph, the carpenter, makes a mousetrap at an upstairs window—outside in the town, people come and go (see left).

### Inventing Oil Paints

Oil was used to keep paint from drying. Details could then be painted with plenty of time. Oil gave the paint a **transparent** appearance. Jan van Eyck was known to have experimented with oils, trying to find a good **varnish.** Oil paintings are usually varnished to add protection. The oil technique was introduced into Italy and gradually became more popular than the usual tempera that was used.

25

# Painting Imagination and Real Life

Some painters in the North illustrated a world of fantasy. But their paintings were inspired by the lives of ordinary people. This love of painting the real world is called **Realism.** It could also help to paint pure imagination and horror.

## Painting Nightmares

The paintings of Hieronymus Bosch (1450–1516), seem to be living nightmares. You could journey around them and stop at every single image to see what horrible thing is going on there. Bosch was making comments on the state of people's souls—on sin and punishment. Human beings are the real subjects of his paintings. Michelangelo was painting only a generation later than Bosch, but he showed people with ideal faces and bodies (see page 20).

For Michaelangelo, even though people might suffer, they lived in a world of beauty. Bosch wanted to show the kind of suffering that might exist in another world—the world of hell.

The left panel of Bosch's *Garden of Earthly Delights* shows a view of paradise. The right-hand panel shows hell. The scene in the central panel is a nightmarish vision of human behavior on Earth.
*The Garden of Earthly Delights*, c. 1500.

A detail from Bosch's view of hell (right-hand panel).

A detail from Bruegel's *Peasant Wedding Feast* (page 27, bottom right).

## Pieter Bruegel

Pieter Bruegel (1525–69), was greatly influenced by Bosch. Like Bosch, he brought fact and fantasy together in wide, far-reaching landscapes. He knew the lives of country people and he liked to paint their humor and sense of fun. His paintings of peasants are filled with dancing colors as figures move about in the foreground. The patterns of their clothes seem to bounce into the background.

Such a love of color and detail is typical of the Northern Renaissance. Italians like Titian (see page 23), wanted to show how they had learned to paint as though the viewer were looking through a window. These two very different styles were being practiced at the end of the sixteenth century in different parts of Europe.

All the people at
Bruegel's *Peasant
Wedding Feast* are
painted as individuals
not as a crowd. These
portraits are of ordinary
people rather than of
rich courtiers.
*Peasant Wedding Feast*,
1568.

A detail from Bruegel's
*Peasant Wedding Feast*
(right).

27

# Rembrandt

Rembrandt van Rijn (1606–69), was born in Leiden in Holland. He was one of nine children. His father was a poor miller. He studied Latin before deciding to move to Amsterdam and be an artist. In Amsterdam Rembrandt married Saskia van Uylenburgh.

## Painting People

Rembrandt was interested in people. He drew people's expressions and made studies of the head and its structure. Rembrandt made thousands of drawings, sketches, and paintings of his own face, over many years. He was able to capture particular expressions, as they passed across the eyes or the corners of the mouth. Rembrandt was asked to paint many wealthy Dutch citizens. Not since Titian (see pages 22–23) had Europe known such a brilliant portrait painter. Rembrandt even painted group portraits. He was able to capture each type of person, the occasion, and the place.

## Painting Light

Rembrandt painted light and shade. To him, color was less important than contrasts of light. Light and its effect was the real subject of his art. An angle, a window, an open page – each had its own kind of light. With such an interest in the drama of light he was happy to make prints because they are made up of shades of black and white. Rembrandt explored his fascination with light even further through etching. Because prints and etchings could be reproduced in large numbers by machines, many were sold and his work became well known all over Europe.

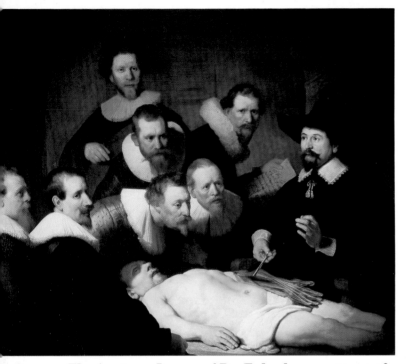

*The Anatomy Lesson of Dr. Tulp* shows a group of well-dressed men standing around a single corpse. Their clean, white ruffs contrast greatly with the decaying flesh of the dead body.
*The Anatomy Lesson of Dr. Tulp*, 1632.

Rembrandt painted many scenes from the Bible. Here, he chose the dramatic moment when, in the middle of a feast, King Belshazzar is warned by God.
*Belshazzar's Feast*, c. 1635.

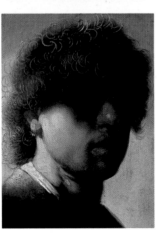

Rembrandt painted himself throughout his life.
*Self-Portrait*, 1632 (right), *Self-Portrait*, c. 1663 (opposite).

This elephant was drawn with soft, black chalk to show its tough skin.
*The Elephant*, 1637.

## Rembrandt and the Church

Rembrandt was living at the time when the Protestant Church had just spread across Europe. Unlike the Catholic Church, it did not **commission** splendid images of Christian stories. Rembrandt was very religious. His own life was struck by the tragic deaths of his wife and young son. His art contains much of this sorrow, his deepest thoughts, and his belief in God.

### Cutting Facts

Engraving is like drawing with a sharp tool on a piece of wood or metal. The picture is cut rather than drawn. In etching, a metal plate is covered in wax then the image is drawn into the wax. Acid is then added to the plate and it eats into the metal, leaving the image clearly cut. There are many stages —often to correct mistakes between the etching and its development into a print. The wooden or metal plate is covered with ink and an impression is made on special paper. The picture has to be drawn the opposite way around to how the artist wants the finished print because the image comes out in reverse when it is printed.

# Indoors and Outdoors

Holland has wide, light, cloud-filled skies above its low, flat land. Rembrandt practiced various light effects in his paintings of landscape. He could paint a distant view where the clouds open and light falls on a single town or village rather like a spotlight. He used his imagination to paint the real world.

A calm river scene has been carefully planned to include the sailing boat, a church, and a tree underneath a vast, sweeping sky.
*A River Landscape,* c. 1645, Jacob van Ruisdael.

A large curtain has been drawn aside in this painting to allow us to see the artist in his studio. Many people think that this is a shy self-portrait as we can only see the artist's back.
*The Painter in his Studio,* 1665/6, Jan Vermeer.

30

## Painting Details

Jan Vermeer (1632–75), painted his home-town Delft, to include every detail. Other artists added their own view of the country. Jacob van Ruisdael (1628/9–82) showed the country as a calm, reassuring place. An evening sunlight moves across the land touching the people and animals who live there. Dutch artists of the seventeenth century were able to make landscape a subject worth painting in its own right, not just as a background to a painting of something else.

## People's Homes

Dutch artists also painted life indoors. We can see homes where people prepare food, read letters, or play music. Vermeer is best known for his interior scenes. Light comes through an open window showing a peaceful, private world, where a few objects are enough to tell us about the house and the people who live there. The Dutch were able to develop their own particular **school** of painting by painting exactly what they saw around them.

A photograph of someone painting in the Dutch countryside.

Dutch artists were concerned with painting people exactly as they were.
*The Young Man and the Old Woman*, 1659–60, Michiel Sweerts (1618–64).

Very often in Dutch interior scenes a door is painted so that it opens up to reveal another room or a view that disappears into the distance.
*A View Down a Corridor*, c. 1662, Samuel van Hoogstraten (1627–78).

31

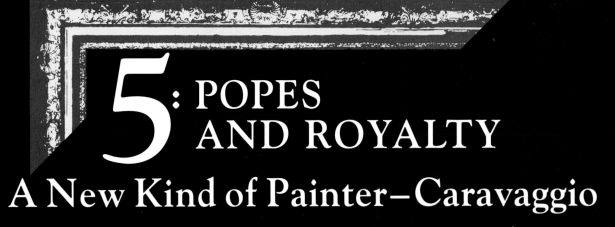

# 5: POPES AND ROYALTY
## A New Kind of Painter–Caravaggio

During the seventeenth century, Europe was a place of great unrest. Christian ideas were changing , which was important for artists who depended on the Church for work. Once again Rome became the center of new ideas in art as it had been during the Renaissance.

### Caravaggio

Caravaggio (1571–1610) came to Rome from northern Italy and shocked everyone with his own kind of realism (see page 26). The Church commissioned his work but his paintings were not immediately liked. It was thought that they did not show enough respect. Caravaggio showed Christian stories taking place in the Rome of his day. Saints look like ordinary people on the streets of Rome. Beggars and wanderers replaced the usual shepherds and kings. Often Caravaggio's people are placed inside the composition as if they are actors. His world is dark with shafts of brilliant light falling inside the scenes to make a drama out of the story he tells. Caravaggio's original ideas were of enormous importance to European artists long after his own death.

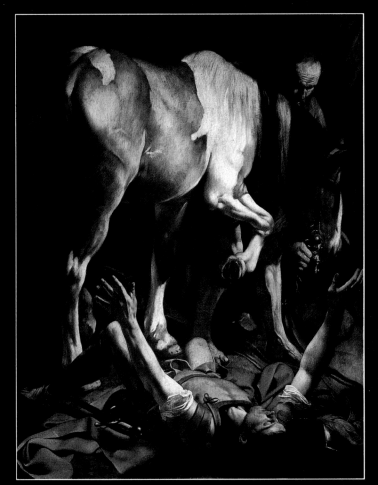

St. Paul is blinded by divine light
Caravaggio, *The Conversion of St. Paul*, 1600-01.

St. Peter is roughly nailed to the cross.
Caravaggio, *The Crucifixion of St. Peter*, 1600-01.

## The Baroque

In Dutch painting you might peep inside a canvas and see someone's private home (see page 31). In Italy you were invited to stop and stare at the splendor of a scene. It was as if the painting was there on purpose to attract you. This style of painting is known as **Baroque** – everything is rather exaggerated. By now painters had mastered the new skills learned during the Renaissance, so they felt they could be daring. The palaces of the popes were light and bright containing stories from mythology or the Bible. Many ceilings were decorated to look like the sky. A person can look into a Roman church or palace and not see a ceiling, but a sky filled with saints, heroes, and angels. These are images of heavenly light very far from Caravaggio's dark world.

**A ceiling painted as if it was a heavenly sky. Andrea Pozzo (1642-1709) *Allegory of the Missionary Work of the Jesuits*, 1691-94.**

# Rubens

Peter Paul Rubens (1577–1640) was not only an artist but a very clever scholar, especially with languages. His job as a Dutch diplomat sent him traveling between countries on royal missions. When he was twenty-three he went to Italy and was able to visit Florence, Venice, and Rome. He was particularly interested in Titian (see pages 22–23) and Michelangelo (see page 20). Rubens returned to the city of Antwerp in 1608.

A map of Europe in Rubens's time (background).

This portrait by Rubens is of his daughter Clara Serena, 1616-17.

## Rubens the Portrait Painter

Rubens was asked to paint a **cycle** on the life of the Italian princess Marie de Medici. Rubens was considered the best artist for such a royal figure, not only because his style of painting suited the subject, but also because of his diplomatic skills. He was able to move easily about Europe and once said "I regard all the

The figures in this painting represent ideas. Peace (center left) is protected from the approach of War (man in armor). Rubens, *Allegory on the Blessings of Peace*, 1629-30.

Charles I (below) encouraged painting and owned many pictures. Van Dyck, *Charles I*, 1635.

world as my country and I believe I should be very welcome everywhere." In 1629 he was knighted by Charles I of England (see right).

Rubens loved painting flesh and the colors of the skin. His brushstrokes were light and assured. Rubens understood all the lessons of Italian art and he added to them his own style of painting.

## Anthony van Dyck

Being so well thought of, Rubens was bound to have pupils. He often did the first sketches of a painting, and the finishing touches, while his pupils did much of the filling-in of the less difficult parts. One of his pupils was Anthony van Dyck (1599–1641). He achieved greatness as a portrait painter with his real feeling for the prestige and power of royalty. Van Dyck was also knighted by Charles I. To be a painter at a European court you had to paint portraits, as this was how royalty was remembered forever. Also, at a time when princes, princesses, and kings and queens from different countries married without having actually met, portraits were carried from country to country as a way of seeing if they liked the look of each other.

35

# Velázquez

The Spanish painter Diego Velázquez's (1599–1660) first paintings were very dark like Caravaggio's (pages 32–33). They were of rough country people and each face was a portrait of a real person. The instruments of people's work, their building tools, or kitchenware, were as carefully painted as their faces. Velázquez painted everyting before him as if it were a still life. Velázquez seems to be there, on the scene, rather like a reporter with a camera recording every detail.

## Royal Painter

In 1623, when he was only twenty-four, Velázquez was made court painter to Philip IV

**Velázquez has painted the young prince on a small pony so that he looks more grand.**
*Prince Carlos,* **1635-36.**

of Spain. Unlike Rubens, who was able to travel around Europe, Velázquez had to stay with the Spanish royal family. He got to know them well and his style changed to suit his new portrait work. He lightened the tone of his paintings and no longer painted a dark world, but his honesty remained. Philip IV was a very ugly man and Velázquez did not pretend that he was handsome. At the Spanish court Velázquez met Rubens who encouraged him to travel to Italy.

## Painting People

Velázquez worked out his own kind of realism (see page 26). He painted the king, the queen, the princes, and the princesses: that was his job. But Velázquez also wanted to paint their servants, especially the dwarfs who were so unlike the other people at the court (see painting below). Velázquez considered them equally interesting and worthwhile subjects for portraiture at a time when only the richest of people had their portraits painted.

Velázquez believed that what the artist saw was the most important thing. Velázquez studied exactly what people looked like so that he could try and reveal their characters when he painted them. Keeping a distance from his subjects, Velázquez was able to explain their real personalities.

*Philip IV,* engraving by an unknown artist.

**Velázquez has included himself in this painting. The princess is attended by maids in this relaxed picture of court life.** ***The Maids of Honor,* 1556.**

# 6:
# PEACE AND REVOLUTION
## A Classical Past

### Back to School

Poussin believed that certain rules should be made for artists to follow. He helped to start an academy in France like the first ones in Italy. Poussin believed that painting should have a serious purpose with a style to match. Many academies existed like small national schools. You had to be a good artist to be able to enter an academy. By studying (below) at an academy you were making art your profession.

Poussin, *Orpheus and Eurydice, 1659.*

Rome has always been an important center of art and has influenced many artists through the ages. While the royal courts of Europe encouraged the Baroque style, two French painters visited Rome and thought about its distant Classical past (see pages 8–9).

## Landscape from the Past

Nicolas Poussin (1594–1665) loved everything he found in Rome – its statues, paintings, music, buildings, and literature. For him, Rome was like a teacher. He liked the quiet order of its art, so unlike the overdramatic art of his own day. The people in his scenes look as though they have come from Ancient Rome. Their movements are grand and elegant – like the figures of Ancient Roman sculpture. His paintings show the ruins that he saw transformed into large, imposing temples and fine cities from many centuries before his lifetime. Bible stories and stories from mythology take place in the same paintings.

## Painting Nature

Like Poussin, Claude Lorrain (1600–82) was French but lived most of his life in Italy. Claude also admired Classical Rome, but he was even more interested in nature and studied the countryside near Rome. There is a dreaminess about his wide, far-reaching landscapes with their gentle sunshine. Light was very important for Claude. He knew that by painting light he could give a picture a certain mood. Many of his scenes are not real views, but imagined ones. Instead of painting one particular scene, artists painted a landscape made up of all the most beautiful parts of the countryside that they could think of. The composition is often framed by trees you can look through to the action. The hills move into the distance one upon the other rather like scenery in the theater. Poussin and Claude both learned from the art of Ancient Rome. They added imagination to what they had learned and painted landscapes that represented an ideal world.

Claude, *Pastoral Landscape with Ponte Molle*, date unknown.

# Rococo Delights

Back in France the people of the royal court decided to enjoy themselves. They wanted art to be lighthearted, not serious or academic. No longer did Classical art or the popes decide what should appear in paintings.

## Painting Love!

Love has always been a popular subject in art. People of the theater, servant-girls, clowns, and traditional characters from mythology were also common subjects for paintings. Women were portrayed as being very feminine – their dresses covered with flowers, their tiny feet dancing. Inspired by Rubens, artists chose to paint men and women **nude.** The Classical style of painting that Poussin had suggested – being carefully thought out with strict rules – was less appealing to them than an image of love and leisure.

Everything in this wood, including the stone statues, seem to reach toward the girl who tosses her slipper to her lover. The scene looks a little unnatural but is still pretty and light.
Jean-Honoré Fragonard (1732-1806), *The Swing*, 1766.

## The Rococo

The word **Rococo** describes this style of painting. Rubens's light brushstrokes and love of color were carried on into the Rococo style. Still life painting was not ignored, nor was portrait painting. But the choice of subjects didn't matter as much. No matter what the subject was it usually became a decorative and pretty picture.

## The End of French Royalty

By the time Louis XVI came to the French throne in 1774, the life of the royal court was all fun and games. Queen Marie Antoinette had a little farm built in the grounds of the Palace of Versailles where she pretended to be a shepherdess. Meanwhile the poverty-stricken French people lived in miserable conditions. Soon the French Revolution would turn society upside down.

### William Hogarth

In England, William Hogarth (1697–1764) criticized the English society in which he lived. He knew that artists could influence people so he created lessons in paint and called them *Modern Moral Subjects*. These pictures are amusing but they are also warnings to people who live foolishly.

**Hogarth illustrates a marriage that will end in unhappiness. The couple's wedding is planned by people who will make money from it.** *Marriage à la Mode,* **1743.**

**Jean-Antoine Watteau (1684-1721) painted fashionable people enjoying themselves in the open air. The** natural setting of their picnic is very different from their lives at home.
*Fête in a Park,* **1718-20.**

**Before the Revolution the French court was a fabulous display of wealth and luxury. This photograph from a movie gives some idea of that lifestyle. Few people in France lived like this.**

# Revolution!

**This woman of the Revolution represents the freedom the French people were fighting for. Eugène Delacroix, *Liberty Leading the People*, 1830.**

Art often changes as events change the world. Sometimes artists rebel against the artistic style of the day. When Pompeii was discovered in the middle of the eighteenth century, Roman culture was once again thought of as the finest in history. In France, the Classical art of Ancient Rome replaced the Rococo.

## David and Ingres

The artist Jacques-Louis David (1748–1825) painted many scenes from ancient history in order to inspire the people of his modern-day France. The figures in his pictures look like figures from Roman sculpture—just like Poussin's (see page 38). David wanted his art to teach everyone who saw it. The subjects he

This painting is of an actual event (right). In order to paint the scene accurately Géricault talked to survivors of the wrecked ship *Medusa* who were lost at sea on a raft for fourteen days.
*The Raft of the Medusa,* 1819.

David was a Classical painter like Ingres. This picture (below) is of the death of Marat, a leader of the revolutionary government who was murdered in his bath.
*The Death of Marat,* 1793.

Despite changing art and politics, Ingres painted in a pure, Classical style (below).
*Bather,* 1808.

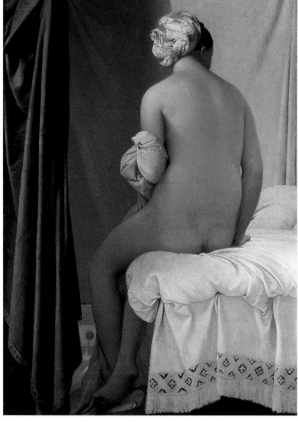

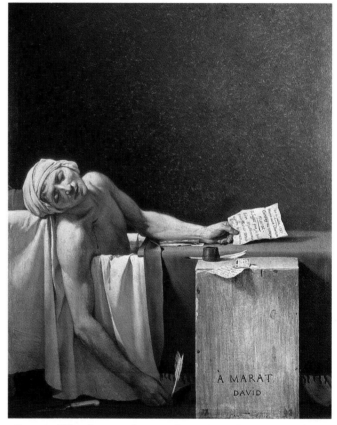

painted represent strict moral ideas. He lived during an uncertain time when civil war was about to break out in France.

Jean-Auguste-Dominique Ingres (1780–1867) was best known for his portraits to which he gave a gracious calm and elegance. To Ingres, drawing was like sculpting a figure on canvas rather than in stone. The pressure of his pencil changed as it steadily moved across the paper, like carving light and shade.

## All Change

The French Revolution of 1789 changed life completely. The king and queen were sent to the **guillotine** to have their heads cut off. The French people felt that without the **monarchy** they were free to govern themselves. Artists like David and Ingres continued to paint as they had always done, but for some artists the new spirit of freedom lived in their paintings. The artists Théodore Géricault (1791–1824), and Eugène Delacroix (1798–1863) often chose subjects that deliberately moved people to think and feel. They painted energetically and were unafraid of showing how their brushes had worked – even if this made their paintings seem rather slapdash.

43

# Goya

Goya painted the Spanish royal family in a very unflattering way (left).
*The Family of Charles IV*, 1800.

*The Colossus* (right), 1808-12.

In 1789, the year of the French Revolution, the Spanish artist Francisco de Goya (1746–1828) went to paint at the court of the king of Spain. Goya knew the work of Velázquez (see pages 36–37) and was also a great portrait painter. Like Velázquez, Goya captured the personality of his subjects without lying about their ugliness or beauty.

## Black and Silver

Goya often used the color black as a contrast to silvery, pale colors in his portraits. He appreciated the dark looks of the Spanish people and painted black lace against flesh colors. His figures often look as though they loom out of the shadows. In 1792 Goya became very ill. When he finally recovered he was completely deaf. He still managed to be an official painter at the court and was always successful and taught at the Spanish Academy. But after his illness Goya's mind was deeply affected. Isolated by his deafness, his dark imagination grew stronger.

## The Horrors of War

Like Bosch (see pages 26–27), Goya was able to paint a nightmare world that seems to have come from his private fears. Twice in his life he produced a series of etchings (see box on page 29). *The Caprices* criticized society and the Church. In *The Disaster of War* he drew some of his imagined terrors as well as some of the terrors of the world he lived in, such as haunting witches, scenes of torture, and people disfigured and injured by war. Goya lived through some of the most turbulent years that Europe has ever known.

In this painting of an actual event Spanish civilians are being shot by French soldiers.
*The Third of May* 1808, 1814.

When Spain was occupied by the French, under Napoleon (1808–14), Goya felt the sorrow of his invaded country. War and darkness absorbed his mind. His painting *The Colossus* (opposite) is of a terrifying giant – is it a giant of evil, a giant fighting to defend itself, or Goya himself, trapped in his soundless world, surrounded by foreign invaders?

44

## The Painter and Poet

William Blake (1757–1827) was an English painter and poet who lived at the same time as Goya. Unlike Goya he had no royal patron to support and commission his work and he remained poor throughout his life. Blake liked to paint on the small scale using watercolors. Most of his work was of illustrations to his own poetry and the Bible. For him, art, imagination, and religion were all one. Blake believed that the world we see is one that hides the world of the imagination and that it is the artist who can reveal it.

**A detail from Blake's *Satan and the Rebel Angels*, 1808.**

# 7: CHANGING LANDSCAPES

# The English Land

What was happening in England? Before the Revolution in France rich Englishmen liked to go on tours abroad as part of their education and to see the artistic talents of other countries. They had no cameras so took artists with them to record their favorite views. John Robert Cozens (1752–97) was an artist who occasionally painted for tourists. His brief studies, done on the spot in moments, were worked into detailed drawings later.

When traveling abroad was no longer easy (because of the French Revolution) the English turned to look at their own land, much the same as the Dutch had done two centuries before (see pages 30–31).

Constable painted this quiet millpond near his home in 1821.
*The Haywain.*

## John Constable

Like the Dutch, John Constable (1776–1837) looked at his home surroundings (the east of England). His oil paintings were often loaded with a thick **impasto** with spots of white to show sparkling sunlight. Constable painted agricultural landscapes where people lived and worked peacefully. He made many studies of clouds, plants, and animals and used them to produce his finished paintings.

## Joseph Mallord William Turner

Turner's (1775–1851) vision of landscape was unlike Constable's. He sensed the power and mystery of nature. His paintings grew out of his immediate impressions. For Turner, the French painter Claude (see pages 38–39) was an inspiration. Throughout his long life, Turner worked at his technique. From tiny sketchbook notes to large paintings filled with dazzling light and color, he tried to show his own feelings about the world.

Artists chose paints and equipment to suit their individual styles. Here is a selection.

Water painted with watercolors, John Sell Cotman (1782-1842), *Greta Bridge*, 1805.

Turner's land- and seascapes are full of movement and enthusiasm for the subject and for painting. *Steamer in a Snowstorm*, 1812.

### Painting with Watercolors

Watercolors have been used for centuries. They are paints that are mixed with water rather than oil or egg, to make a very fluid paint. They dry quickly and are well suited to open-air sketching.

# The French Land

## The Barbizon School

The French were also painting landscapes. In the mid-1840s a few painters gathered together to explore the forest of Fontainebleau. They called themselves the Barbizon school, after the village where they stayed. Each artist painted what he liked best in the forest. Théodore Rousseau (1812–67), the leader of the group, was influenced by the Dutch and by Constable. He loved to paint the grandeur and individual character of trees. The Barbizon

Women are bending to pick stubble off the fields after the harvest. Millet has painted warm light into the picture which gives their tough work a quiet dignity.
Jean-François Millet, *The Gleaners*, 1857.

Detail from *The Stonebreakers*, 1849.

painters drew the forest they saw, without adding or subtracting any feature for the sake of a good composition. They spent much time out of doors, studying and sketching, but had to finish their oil paintings indoors.

Jean-François Millet (1814–75) painted the peasants whose life was hard (above). Poor country folk were not usually thought of as a suitable subject for painting. Millet and the Barbizon school wanted to escape such academic rules. The ordinary working people in his paintings are shown leading quiet, simple lives close to nature.

## Painting the Real World

Gustave Courbet (1819–77) was not a member of the Barbizon school but was very influenced by their work. Courbet included ugliness in his work, such as animals killing each other. In Paris he made himself heard – criticizing all the art that had Rome and an ideal past as its roots or subject. For Courbet, art had to imitate real life and be of the present day not the past. When Courbet was asked to paint an angel in a church painting, he said "I have never seen angels. Show me an angel and I will paint one."

Camille Corot traveled to Rome to examine its ruins. In this picture of Chartres Cathedral in France Corot showed the stones and houses in soft sunlight. Corot was later much influenced by the Barbizon school. *Chartres Cathedral*, 1830.

Rousseau was disappointed by town life and preferred to live in the country where he "understood the language of the forests." *Holm Oaks*, 1855, Apremont.

The real world was the subject of the art of these painters. They went outside to find out what was happening in the countryside, who was there, and what they were doing.

Stonebreaking was one of the hardest jobs of all but Courbet chose it for the subject of one of his most famous paintings. Detail from *The Stonebreakers*, 1849.

# Monet and The Impressionists

Courbet and Millet's fresh look at landscape painting was about to lead to a revolution in art.

The Impressionists dared to try a new painting technique that suited their needs. Just as Turner had spread unmixed color onto his canvases to make them look brilliant, so the Impressionists painted straight from the tube (see box). They did not try to disguise their brushstrokes. They saw a flicker of sunlight and they captured that light in a quick "daub" of color. Often this meant that a painting looked unfinished – as if a drawing had been patchily covered. The Impressionists were aware of this. They wanted to re-create the sensation of a scene, as if the canvas was an idea or feeling in paint.

## Painting from Tubes

The invention of the tube of paint in 1841 changed methods of painting completely. Now artists could mix their colors on the spot, out of doors. Tubes were portable and practical. The Impressionists could capture changing weather conditions much more easily and quickly, with their ready-mixed paints.

50

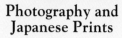

## Photography and Japanese Prints

When the Impressionists were painting in Paris in the 1860s many things influenced the way they worked. Japanese art and the invention of photography were two very important influences.

The Impressionists saw the art of Japan in the cheap mass-produced prints that were exported all over Europe and America with goods such as tea. Artists like Monet and Degas loved the strange off-center Japanese composition and plain colors. Degas especially used some of these colorings and compositions in his work.

Photography became more widely available in 1839. Painters had always had to paint portraits, important events, and landscapes because painting and drawing were the only ways of recording things – stopping them in time. When photography came along painters soon realized that they no longer had to paint anything in particular, or try to make what they painted look real because cameras could do the same job more accurately. Artists were now more free to use their imaginations and paint anything in whatever way they wished.

## Rebelling Against Society

Since their work was unpopular and the official school of art would not show it, they set up their own exhibitions. The first, in 1874, included a picture by Claude Monet (1840–1926), called *Impression, Sunrise.* It shows his first response to the sun rising over the docks of Le Havre, a French port on the English Channel. It was badly criticized but gave Monet and his friends a group name – The Impressionists.

## Renoir and Monet

Auguste Renoir (1841–1919), like Rubens (see page 34), loved to paint red tints of flesh and the soft textures of cloth. All his works are painted with a light and feathery touch.

Monet especially, of all the Impressionists, wanted to show the effects of light in his painting. He studied the same subject – the front of Rouen Cathedral, poplar trees, haystacks – to see how light changed their appearance at different times of the day. In the end they became less of an object, more a patch or shape of shimmering color, shadow, and light.

The Impressionists succeeded in changing old ideas and inventing a new and modern art.

Unlike most of the Impressionists, Edgar Degas (1834–1917) painted indoor scenes and was especially fond of painting in theaters.
*Fin d'arabesque (Ballet Dancer),* 1877.

# Painting the Colors of the Sun

Both Gauguin (inset) and Van Gogh (right) painted portraits of themselves. *Self-Portrait*, 1888, Paul Gauguin, (inset). *Self-Portrait*, 1889, Vincent van Gogh, (right).

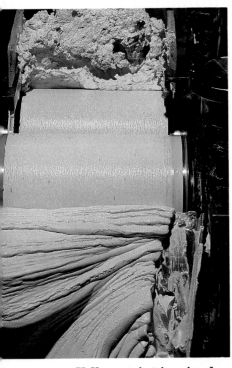

Yellow paint is mixed between the rollers of a machine. The color is then put into tubes (see box on page 50). The Impressionists and Postimpressionists used paint straight from the tube to make their work look very bright.

We often recognize things because of their colors – the sky is blue and the grass is green. The Impressionists helped artists to think more about color as a very important and more exciting part of painting.

## Painting a Mountain

At this time, toward the end of the last century, many people were thinking about art in a scientific way, much as the early Renaissance Italians had worked out problems of perspective (see page 17). Paul Cézanne (1839–1906) was interested in the structure of things. He spent years in the heat and bright sunlight of Provence in the south of France, painting the same mountain from many sides, in different weather conditions. For him it was important not to show nature as something that was looked at quickly, but as part of a timeless and unchanging world.

## Two Friends, Van Gogh and Gauguin

Vincent van Gogh (1853–90), came to Paris from his native Holland. He was influenced by the Impressionists' work and changed the colors of his paintings from dark scenes to sun-filled ones. He also wanted to live in Provence, with a group of artists who shared the same artistic thoughts. His brushstrokes seem fierce and heavy with paint. He worked quickly, loading the canvas with brilliant colors in "daubs" that almost make the outlines of subjects move.

Van Gogh invited Paul Gauguin (1848–1903) to join him in the south of France. Gauguin was a difficult man to live with. He was ready to give up his wife, children, friends, and country for his art. He moved to a faraway tropical island where he worked out the ideas he had formed in France. Colors were important to him in their own right, and could turn a canvas into many decorative patterns. Gauguin's paintings show how the Renaissance discovery of perspective and the use in painting of light and shade – that had been in the minds of artists for centuries – were no longer essential to modern artists.

**A photograph of Mont Sainte-Victoire, the mountain Cézanne painted again and again.**

**One of Cézanne's images of Mont Sainte-Victoire in Provence in the south of France.** *Mont Ste-Victoire* **1890–95.**

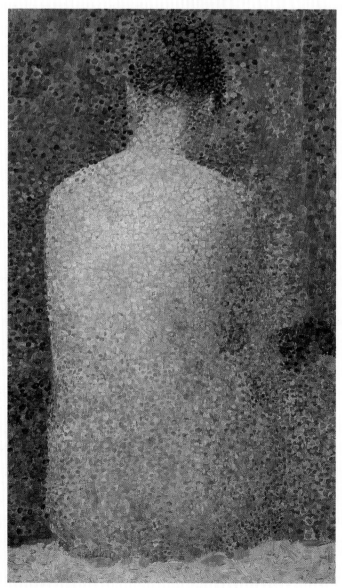

**Georges Seurat painted images made up of tiny blocks or spots of color.** *Back of a Nude Woman,* **1887, Georges Seurat (1859–91).**

53

# 8: THE MODERN WORLD

## Picasso and Other Wild Beasts

### Art of the Modern World

By the start of this century, life for everyone was changing fast. Electricity replaced fire and steam. Soon airplanes would soar into the sky. Art explains much about how people live. The beginning of the twentieth century saw artists being more inventive than ever.

### Wild Beasts

Color was important to a new group of artists who were nicknamed Fauves or Wild Beasts at their first exhibition in Paris in 1905. They were told their paintings looked like children's. Henri Matisse (1869–1954) believed that you should paint in the same way that you did as a child. He liked the bright, bold paintings of Van Gogh and Gauguin.

Matisse was a master of color. Matisse drew with color rather than with black lines. By putting certain colors next to each other the artist makes this painting look as though it is shimmering with heat on a summer's day.
*Open window at Collioure,* a Fauve work of 1905.

### Abstract Art

Abstract art is art that does not imitate nature and the world around us. This type of art had its beginnings before the twentieth century. Photography and movies were able to show what the real world looks like. Artists could think of other ways of seeing–sometimes with an appreciation of color, line, and shape alone. In 1910 in Germany, the Russian painter Wassily Kandinsky (1866–1944) produced a style of painting that shocked the public. His paintings did not seem to represent anything that was easy to recognize. This is called abstract art. Since 1910 abstract art has become much more familiar.

*Guernica* is Picasso's painting of the Spanish town of Guernica at the moment at which it was bombed during the Spanish civil war in 1937. *Guernica* shows one of the many styles Picasso worked in.

Kandinsky believed that different colors make people react in certain ways. For instance, he thought that something painted in red acted like a command. Originally, Kandinsky called his abstract paintings "color music." *Cossacks*, 1910–11.

This painting by Picasso illustrates his Cubist style. The violin has been taken apart and put back together again in a slightly different order. *The Violin*, 1911–12.

## Cubism

Paul Cézanne said we should find the shapes of the sphere, the cone, and the cylinder in nature. He did not imagine that his ideas would lead to a new type of painting known as Cubism.

The Spanish painter Pablo Picasso (1881–1973) was the leader of Cubism. At the beginning of his long and inventive artistic career Picasso worked closely with the French painter Georges Braque (1882–1963). They experimented with painting unusual views of objects. Picasso and Braque often used **collage.** At times it became difficult to see the real subject of their paintings because of their distorted viewpoints.

A spirit of adventure was felt by many artists. Marcel Duchamp (1887–1968) painted the *Nude Descending a Staircase* at every point of her journey like a clockwork toy. He wanted to show movement, not just one particular moment frozen in time.

Marcel Duchamp, *Nude Descending a Staircase,* 1913 (see also pages 56–57).

55

# Dada and Dreams

## What Is Art?

During World War I (1914–18) people were made very aware of the evil humans are capable of. Goya had felt this too (see pages 44–45), but life was no longer like eighteenth-century Spain. In the cafés of Zurich (Switzerland) artists met, watched **cabarets,** and wrote poems. They wanted to produce art that could shock people – just as the war was shocking. They called their art Dada. This name was chosen at random but is in fact the French word for a child's hobby horse.

Art need not be by individual artists, but by groups of artists like the workshops of the ancient Greeks. Art could be nothing but a pile of rubbish collected from the streets. When the glass of one of Duchamp's paintings broke, he left it like that – to its own fate – rather than replace it. The Dada artists had their own unusual artistic ideas that were very "anti-art." This means that their ideas of art were not the same as the rest of society's – they were rebelling in the same kind of way as the Impressionists had but their work looks very different.

## Futurists

At the beginning of this century the world was changing very rapidly. Cars, airplanes, fast ships, and motorcycles were all new inventions carrying people across the ground, through the air, and over the sea faster than ever before.

In Milan (Italy) in 1909, the Italian poet Filippo Marinetti (1876–1944) published an article in a daily newspaper calling on artists everywhere to become Futurists. Marinetti wanted artists to stop painting historical events in old-fashioned styles. Instead he wanted artists to paint the movement, machinery, speed, and violence of the new century. Several Italian artists joined Marinetti and they traveled all over Europe performing cabarets about their art, painting pictures, and shouting poetry.

Futurism is another example of how art can reflect the world that surrounds it and can also try to change it.

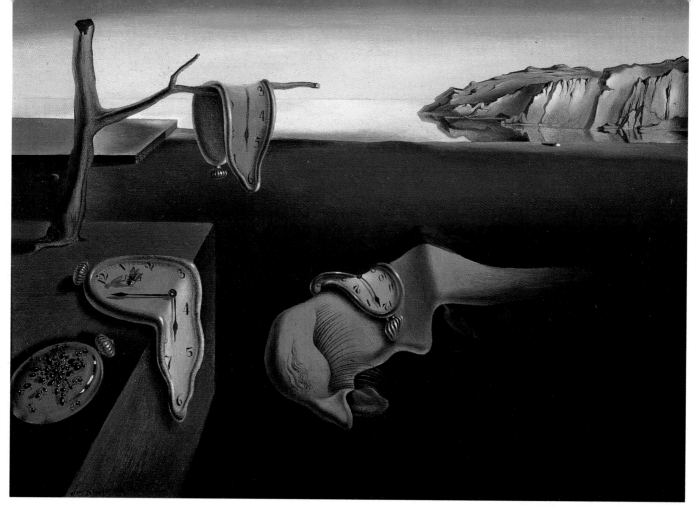

A strange clock drips off the edge of a table in an unfriendly landscape. As in dreams, familiar things are transformed in Dali's Surreal world.
*The Persistence of Memory,* 1931.

## Painting Dreams

At the beginning of the century the study of **psychology,** the working of the mind, was making progress. All that is **irrational** – dreams, behavior, memory – are part of a person. Bosch and Goya had painted nightmare scenes. Now, helped by the psychologists' work, artists painted a dream world.

The Belgian artist René Magritte (1898– 1967) painted rocks floating in the air and fish with legs. His landscapes contain the objects of memories. Many emotions – but particularly those that cannot be controlled – were shown in this **Surreal** art. Salvador Dali (1904–89), a Spanish painter, asked himself many questions – what is the state of the world now? What do people know for sure? Realism does not mean only the things we see with our eyes. The brain hides all sorts of other strange worlds.

By taking manufactured objects and exhibiting them as art, Duchamp questioned people's idea of what art is. In this image he put together two objects in unexpected combination.
Marcel Duchamp, *Pocket Chess Set with Rubber Glove,* 1942.

Derby-hatted men seem to rain from the sky in one of Magritte's dreamlike images (left).
A detail from *Golconde,* 1953.

# New Frontiers – America

When World War II broke out, many European artists fled to the United States. American and European artists found a new freedom as this country thrived over the following years.

## Action and Color

The American artist Jackson Pollock (1912–56) was an Action painter. Pollock became physically involved with his paintings as a way of expressing his feelings, often painting with his hands. The canvas might be smothered with drips of paint or he might even ride a bicycle over its wet surface (see above right).

Unlike Pollock, Mark Rothko (1903–70), turned his large canvases into realms of space and color (opposite). His work can be compared to the brilliant natural world of Turner (see page 47).

Jackson Pollock's paintings shocked the public because he left the final appearance of the picture to chance by splashing and dripping paint over the canvas.
*Yellow Island*, 1952.

ALTHOUGH HE HOLDS HIS BRUSH AND PALETTE IN HIS HANDS, I KNOW HIS HEART IS ALWAYS WITH ME!

Roy Lichtenstein turned throwaway comic strip pictures into art by enlarging them on canvas and making them permanent images (left).
(1923- ), *Girl at Piano.*

Rothko's work is called Color Field painting because it concentrates on the effect colors have on the person looking at the painting (above).
*Red on Maroon*, 1959.

## What's Next?

Communication in modern times knows very few limits. We can write, telephone, and **fax** each other across the world. Television and newspapers spread the news. Photography snaps real life and action.

Prehistoric people knew that bison stalked the land outside their caves. Modern people see the world through television. Why human beings should want to turn what they see, know, or feel into art is not easy to explain. But as long as we have eyes to see, art is certain to continue and who knows what will be created next?

Andy Warhol, *Marilyn Diptych*, 1962 (right).

## Pop Art

In the 1960s the music of the Beatles was heard throughout the world. Art could also become Pop like music. Pop art welcomed the images we see around us every day, such as cans of Coke, newspaper advertisements, and comic strips. When the American artist Andy Warhol (1928–1987) printed a photograph of Marilyn Monroe over and over again, he was trying to show that anything in modern life can be made into art and that art is a mechanical process in which a single image can be produced repeatedly.

# Glossary

## A

**aboriginal**: an aboriginal is the earliest proven human inhabitant of a country or area. Commonly, we refer to the original inhabitants of Australia as Aborigines.

**Adoration of the Shepherds**: the title given to the scene from the Bible where the shepherds go and offer their gifts to the baby Jesus in the stable of his birth in Bethlehem.

**allegory**: a story that has a hidden meaning or means something entirely different from its obvious appearance.

**Annunciation**: the name given to the scene from the Bible where the angel Gabriel appears to the Virgin Mary and tells her that she will give birth to Jesus.

**apostle**: one of the original twelve followers of Jesus who went on to preach Christianity after Christ's death.

**archaeologist**: someone who discovers information about the past by digging for and examining objects that have survived from other periods of time.

## B

**Baroque**: the name given to some art of the seventeenth century. Any art which is elaborate, fussy, or theatrical can be referred to as Baroque. It originated in France and gradually became popular all over Europe.

## C

**c.**: circa, or approximately, usually used with a date.

**cabaret**: a cabaret is a show that is staged in a restaurant. The cabaret usually consists of several different acts instead of just one performer. Cabaret acts can range from singing and dancing to circus tricks.

**Classical**: the name given to any art that has the features of the Ancient Greek Classical period of culture (late 4th-1st century B.C.) or Classical Roman art up until the second century A.D.

**collage**: a **technique** in art where objects such as photographs, bits of cloth, or newspaper cuttings are stuck onto a canvas.

**commissioned**: when somebody commissions a work of art they pay the artist to produce a work for a special place with definite instructions as to size and subject.

**composition**: the name given to the way elements of a painting are arranged by the artist. The use of color, the artist's viewpoint, and the size of the canvas can all affect the composition.

**cycle**: a series of paintings on the same theme or subject located in the same place.

## D

**d.**: died, usually given with year of death.

**decorative**: something that is very attractive and beautifully and richly ornamented.

## F

**fax**: a machine that can transmit written information around the world by using phone lines.

**foreground**: the area at the front of a scene. The foreground is the opposite of the background.

## G

**guillotine**: the machine used during the French Revolution (1789) to execute people. The guillotine consisted of a sharpened blade that was pulled to a certain height above someone's neck. The blade would then be released and would chop the person's head off.

## I

**icon**: an image that comes to represent an idea; in art, a religious image.

**ideal**: when something (such as a body or a landscape) is called ideal it means that it is considered to be perfect. Ideals are not always the same from one period to another. Different people consider different things to be ideal.

**illusion**: something which looks real but is not.

**impasto**: the name given to the effect that is created when paint is put thickly onto the canvas.

60

A detail from Claude Lorrain's *Pastoral Landscape with Ponte Molle* (right), the date is unknown. The whole picture can be seen on pages 38-39.

**interior**: the inside of something.

**irrational**: not reasonable; something that doesn't make sense.

# M

**mammoth**: the mammoth was a very large relative of the elephant. We do not know why the mammoth became extinct thousands of years ago.

**memorial**: a piece of writing that is composed or a piece of art that is made in order to remember the dead. A memorial can say many things such as how long someone lived, where they lived, or what they did during their lifetime.

**monarchy**: A nation that is ruled by a single person who usually inherits the position.

**mosaic**: a picture that is made up of many small pieces of colored marble, pottery, or glass fitted together.

**mythology**: traditional stories of gods, goddesses, heroes, and heroines. Very often myths tell stories with hidden meaning rather like **allegories.**

# N

**Nativity**: the name given to the scene from the Bible where Jesus is born in a stable in Bethlehem surrounded by kings, shepherds, and animals.

**nude**: a representation of an unclothed person; a favorite subject of many artists.

# P

**patron**: someone who supports the arts by **commissioning** artists and sculptors to work for him or her.

**persecuted**: to be persecuted is to be hunted down and punished for what one believes in (usually for religious or political reasons).

**perspective**: to draw something in perspective is to show it exactly as it appears in real life. When something is drawn in perspective it looks as though it has real depth and recedes into the distance.

**polyptych**: an altarpiece which is made up of four or more panels that are hinged and can close together.

**prehistoric**: a period of history that happened before human beings made written records.

**psychology**: the study of the workings of the mind, behavior, and attitudes of human beings. The science of psychology was founded by the psychiatrists Sigmund Freud and Carl Jung at the turn of the century.

# R

**Realism**: the name given to paintings that try to show the world exactly as it is even if that means drawing unpleasant or unattractive things.

**Renaissance**: the period of European history from the early fifteenth to the mid-sixteenth centuries. Renaissance means "rebirth" in French and marks the change from the Middle Ages to the Modern Age. The rebirth refers to the revival of arts, literature, politics, trade, sciences, and medicine.

**Rococo**: the name given to a style of art that was popular in Europe during the early eighteenth century. Art and architecture that is Rococo looks quite playful, light, and graceful.

# S

**school**: sometimes, when a group of artists get together, influence each other, and paint in the same style or use similar subjects during the same period of time they are called a school.

**sinopia**: the name of a reddish-brown chalk used to sketch out a fresco on a wall; a preliminary drawing for a fresco.

**still life**: a picture consisting of inanimate objects arranged together.

**Surrealism**: a type of art that started in France in the 1920s. Surrealism spread all over Europe especially into Germany and Spain. Surrealists tried to paint the unknown world of the mind, dreams, and the **irrational.** The Surrealists were interested in **psychology.**

# T

**technique**: the process or practice that is used to obtain a particular artistic effect. There are many techniques in painting that are taught in art schools such as how to paint with watercolors and how to paint with oils.

**tempera**: a paint made up of water, egg, and color that was commonly used until the **Renaissance** and is still used today.

**three-dimensional**: when something is three-dimensional it is made up of the three dimensions of length, breadth, and depth. Sculpture is three-dimensional.

**tone**: the appearance of light and shade in a painting or drawing.

**transparent**: fine or clear enough to be seen through, like glass.

**two-dimensional**: when something is two-dimensional it exists in only two dimensions. For example, the flat surface of a piece of paper has length and breadth but no depth.

# V

**varnish**: a liquid that when spread on a surface dries to form a hard, shiny, thin, **transparent** coating. Since the Middle Ages it has been common practice for artists to cover their newly completed paintings with a varnish in order to protect the work. Sometimes, varnish is mixed with paint to make it shine.

**Vatican**: the Vatican is the home of the pope who is the leader of the Roman Catholic faith. The Vatican is not just one building or church but is an entire city in the middle of Rome (Italy) with its own postal system and police.

**vault**: an arched roof or ceiling, usually of masonry.

A detail from Nicolas Poussin's *Orpheus and Eurydice* of 1659. The entire picture can be found on page 38.

# Further Reading

Arenas, Jose. *The Key to Renaissance Art.* Lerner, 1990

Blizzard, Gladys. *Come Look with Me: Exploring Landscape Art with Children.* Thomasson-Grant, 1992

Cook, J. *Understanding Modern Art.* Usborne, 1992

Cush, Cathie. *Artists Who Created Great Works,* "20 Events" series. Raintree Steck-Vaughn, 1995

Greenberg, Jan and Jordon, Sandra. *The Sculptor's Eye: Looking at Contemporary Art.* Delacorte, 1993

Keightley, Moy. *Investigating Art: A Practical Guide for Young People.* Facts on File.

Lace, William W. *Michelangelo.* Lucent, 1993

Muhlberger, Richard. *What Makes a Rembrandt a Rembrandt?* Viking, 1993

Plain, Nancy. *Mary Cassatt: An Artist's Life.* Macmillan, 1994

Sills, Leslie. *Visions: Stories about Women Artists.* Albert Whitman, 1993

Sullivan, Charles, ed., *Children of Promise: African-America Literature and Art for Young People.* Abrams, 1991

# Index

A **bold** number indicates that the entry is illustrated on that page. A word in **bold** can be found in the glossary on pages 60–62.

**aboriginal** art 5
abstract art 54–**55**
academies and schools of painting **38**, 44, 51
**allegory** 23
altarpieces **14–15**, 17, 24, **25**
American art **58–59**
animals, portrayal of 4, 6, **8**, 9, 19, 49

background in paintings 26, 31
**Baroque** 33, 39
Bellini, Giovanni 22, **23**
Bible scenes **28**, 39, 45
Blake, William **45**
*Book of Kells* **11**
books, manuscripts **11**, 24
Bosch, Hieronymus **26–27**, 44, 57
Braque, Georges 55
Bruegel, Pieter **26–27**
brushes 4, 43, 47, 50, 53
Byzantine art 10, 12, **13**

Caravaggio **32**, 36
ceiling 10, **20**, 21, **33**
Cézanne, Paul **53**, 55
Charles I of England **35**
Christian art 10–15, 20–21, 24–**25**, 32–33
churches and chapels 10, 12–13, 14, 17, 24, 33
Claude Lorrain **38–39**, 47
**collage** 55
color 15, 22, 26, 28, 41, 44, 47, 50, 51, 52–53, 54–55, 58
**commissioning** of paintings, 29, 45
**composition** 13, 18, 39
Constable, John **46**, 47, 48
Corot 49
Cotman, John Sell 47
Courbet, Gustave **48–49**, 50
Cozens, John Robert 46
Cubism 55

Dada 56, **57**
Dali, Salvador **57**
David, Jacques-Louis 42–43
da Vinci, Leonardo **18–19**
**decorative** art, 41, 53
Degas, Edgar **51**

Delacroix, Eugène 42–43
del Verrochio, Andrea 18
Duccio **13**, **14–15**
Duchamp, Marcel **55**, 56, 57
Dürer, Albrecht **25**

England and English art 41, 45, **46–47**
engravings **25**, 29, **36–37**
etchings 25, 28, 29, 44

Fauves **54**
Florence 12, 14, 16–17, 18, 24, 34
Fontainebleau 48
**foreground** in paintings 15
Fragonard, Jean-Honoré **40**
France and French painting **38–39**, **40**, 41, **42–43**, **48–49**, **50–53**, **54–55**, 57
French Revolution **41**, **42–43**, 44, 46
frescoes 8–**9**, 10, **12–13**, **16**, 17, 23, 24
Futurism 56

Gauguin, Paul **52–53**, 54
Gentile da Fabriano **15**
geometric designs 4, **6**
Géricault, Théodore **43**
Germany and German art 24–**25**

Giorgione **23**
Giotto **12–13,** 14
Goya, Francisco de **44–45,** 56, 57
Gozzoli, Benozzo **16** and also detail on cover
Greek art, ancient 6–**7,** 8, 18, 56

hands, fingers, painting with **4–5,** 58
Hogarth, William **41**
Holland and Dutch painting **24–25, 26–27, 28–29, 30–31,** 33, **34–35,** 46, 48, **52–53**
Hoogstraten, Samuel van **31**
human body, portrayal of 6–**7, 13, 17, 19, 20, 31, 35, 42–43, 48,** 51

**icons** 10
**ideal** 8, **39**
**illusion** 9, **33**
imaginative art **26–27, 39,** 44, **45**
**impasto** 46, **50**
Impressionism **50–51, 52–53,** 56
Ingres, Jean-Auguste-Dominique **42–43**
**interiors** 8, 9, **31**
Italy and Italian art **12–23, 32–33,** 56

Japanese art 51

Kandinsky, Wassily 54–**55**

landscapes 17, 19, 22, 26, **30–31, 38–39, 46–47, 48–49,** 50, 51
Lascaux, caves of 4
Lichtenstein, Roy **58**
light 19, 22, 23, 28, 30, 32, 39, 43, 47, 48, 50, 51
love, portrayal of **40**

Magritte, René **56,** 57
Manet, Edouard **50**
Mantegna, Andrea **17**
Marinetti, Filippo 56
Master of Flémalle **25**
Matisse, Henri **54**
Medici family 16–**17,** 18, 34

medieval art **10–11**
Michelangelo Buonarrotti 18, **20,** 21, 26, 34
Millet, Jean-François **48,** 50
modern art **54–58**
monasteries 11
Monet, Claude **51**
**mosaics** 8, 9, 10
**mythology** 6–7, 8–9, 39, 40

**nude** in art 40, 53

paint 4, 8, 9, 14, 25, 46, 47, 50, 52, 53
**patrons** 17, 18, **20,** 21, **36–37,** 45
Pêch-Merle, caves of **4, 5**
**perspective 17,** 53
Philip IV of Spain **36–37**
photography 31, 51, 54, 58
Picasso, Pablo **54–55**
Pliny the Elder 8–**9,** 24
Pollock, Jackson **58**
**polyptych** 24
Pompeii **8–9,** 42
Pop art **58, 59**
popes 20–21, 32–33, 40
portraits **22,** 24, 27, 28–29, **34,** 36–37, 41, 43, 44, 50, 51, **52**
Postimpressionism **52–53**
pottery **6–7,** 8–9
Poussin, Nicholas **38–39,** 40, 42
Pozzo, Andrea 33
**prehistoric** art **4–5**
prints 28

Raphael **20, 21**
**Realism 26–27,** 37, **49,** 57
Rembrandt van Rijn **28–29**
**Renaissance 16–23, 24–25,** 26, 32, 33, 53
Renoir, Auguste 51
rock paintings **4–5**
**Rococo 40–41,** 42
Roman art **8–9,** 18, 39, 42
Rome 20, 32, 34, 39, 42
Rothko, Mark **58**

Rousseau, Théodore 48–**49**
Rubens, Peter Paul **34–35,** 37, 40, 41, 51
Ruisdael, Jacob van **30–31**
Russian painting 54–**55**

sculpture 7, 39, 42, 43
Seurat, Georges **53**
*sfumato* **18,** 19
**sinopia** 13, 61
Sistine Chapel **20,** 21
Spain and Spanish art **36–37, 44, 55, 56**
stained glass **10**
**still life** 9, 36, 41
**Surrealism 57**

**technique** 25
**tempera** 14, 25, 62
Tintoretto, Jacopo **22–23**
Titian **22,** 26, 28, 34
**tone** 19, 37
*trompe l'oeil* 9
Turner, Joseph Mallord William **47,** 50, 58

Uccello, Paolo **17**

van Dyck, Anthony **35**
van Eyck, Jan **24,** 25
van Gogh, Vincent **52–53,** 54
**varnish** 25
Vasari, Giorgio **17**
**Vatican 20, 21**
Velázquez, Diego **36–37,** 44
Venice **22–23,** 34
Vermeer, Jan **30–31**

wall paintings **4** (see also frescoes)
Warhol, Andy **59**
watercolor painting **45,** 47
Watteau, Jean-Antoine **41**
woodcuts **25**

Zurich 56